BERTHA TAKES A DRIVE

How the Benz Automobile Changed the World

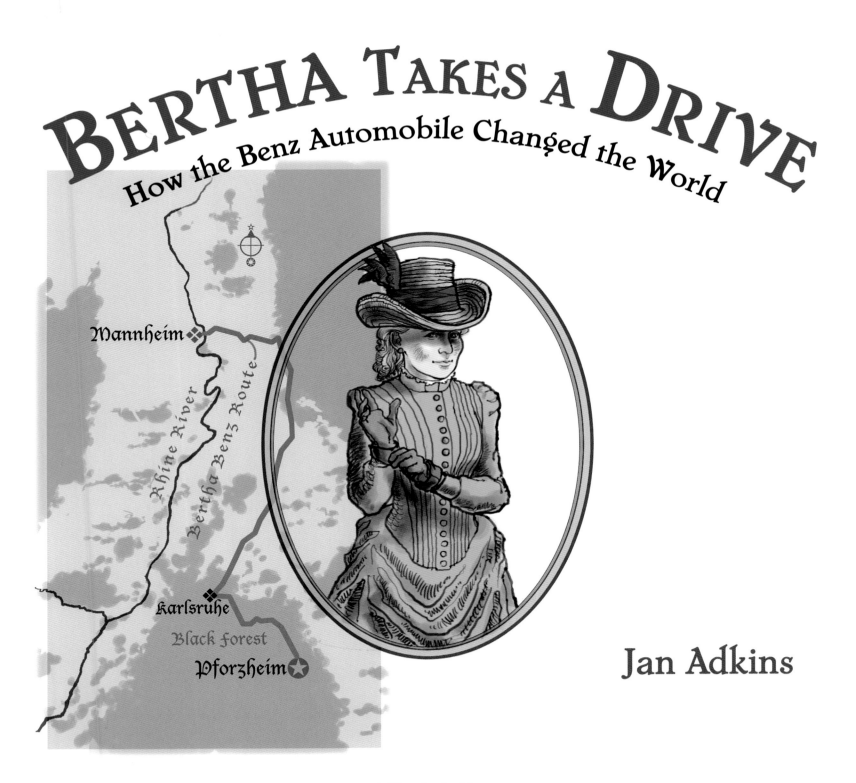

Mannheim

Rhine River

Bertha Benz Route

Karlsruhe

Black forest

Pforzheim

Jan Adkins

Charlesbridge

This book, and the love of our little family in Gainesville,
is for our marvelous new member, Gloria Zinnia Burger.

Published by Charlesbridge
85 Main Street
Watertown, MA 02472
(617) 926-0329
www.charlesbridge.com

Library of Congress Cataloging-in-Publication Data
Adkins, Jan, author, illustrator.
Bertha takes a drive / [author and illustrator] Jan Adkins.
        pages cm
    ISBN 978-1-58089-696-2 (reinforced for library use)
    ISBN 978-1-60734-754-5 (ebook)
    ISBN 978-1-60734-709-5 (ebook pdf)
1. Automobile travel—Germany—History—19th century—Juvenile literature.
2. Benz, Bertha, 1849–1944—Juvenile literature. 3. Automobiles—Germany—
History—19th century—Juvenile literature. 4. Mercedes automobiles—
History—Juvenile literature.
I. Title.
GV1025.G3A113 2015
796.70943—dc23   2014010488

Printed in China
(hc) 10 9 8 7 6 5 4 3 2 1

The illustrations were done in Photoshop on an iMac using a Wacom Pro pressure-sensitive pad
    and a Pantone Matching System CMYK "solid coated" palette.
Display type set in Chesterfield LT STD by Linotype Library GmbH
Text type set in Adobe Caslon Pro by Adobe Systems
Color separations by Colourscan Print Co Pte Ltd, Singapore
Printed by 1010 Printing International Limited in Huizhou, Guangdong, China
Production supervision by Brian G. Walker
Designed by Martha MacLeod Sikkema

Bertha Benz woke her two oldest children with a soft nudge. She put a finger to her lips. "Quiet," she whispered.

All three tiptoed down the stairs in their socks. They put on their shoes and stepped into Papa's shop.

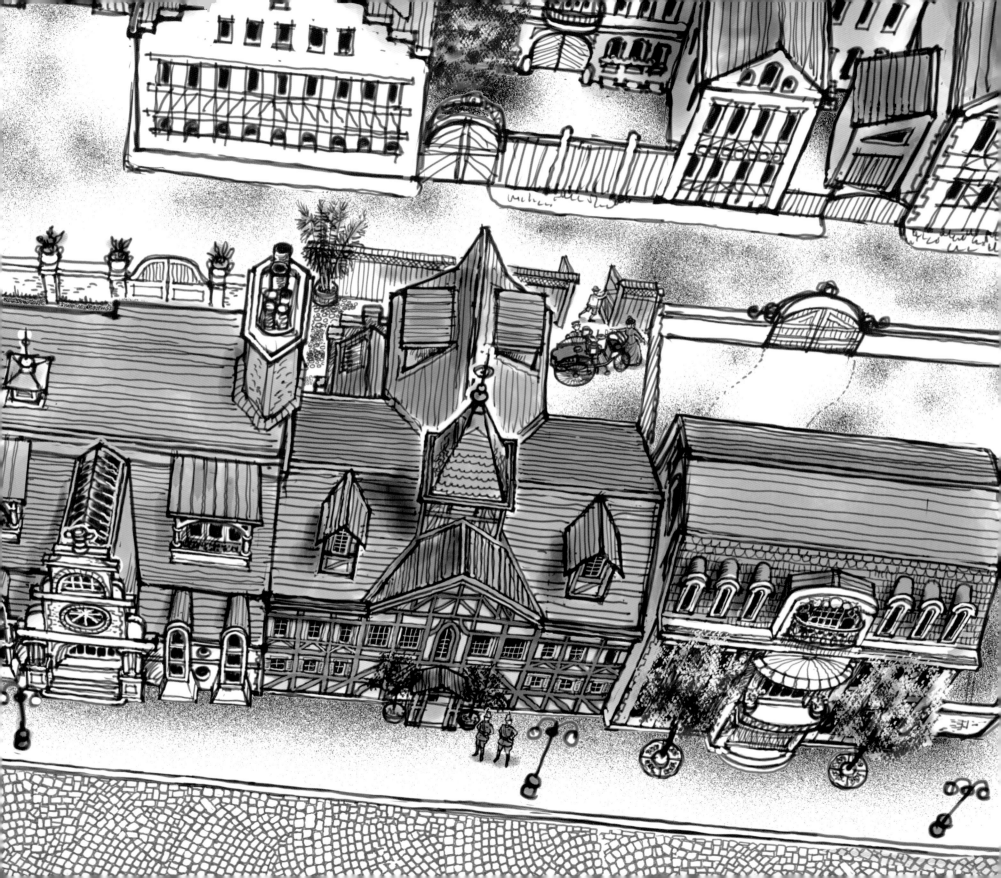

In the cool August morning, Bertha, Richard, and Eugen pushed a strange machine out of the shop and into the alley. They were sneaking away with Papa's invention: the Benz Motorwagen!

Richard began to giggle.

"Hush," Bertha whispered. "The policemen out front will hear you."

Germany's emperor, Wilhelm II, had declared the Motorwagen illegal and posted two officers outside the Benzes' home. The government couldn't imagine what would happen if people could get up and go wherever they wanted, whenever they wanted.

Church officials were not happy with the invention, either. It was too new and too loud. They called it *der Teufelwagen*—the Devil's Wagon.

But Bertha was convinced the Motorwagen could be wonderful. At the end of the alley, she gave the engine's big flywheel a spin. It started up smoothly and quietly.

"Where are we going?" Richard asked.

"To Grandmother's," said Bertha.

"To Pforzheim!" Eugen exclaimed. He and Richard could hardly believe it. Grandmother's house was more than sixty miles away. The Motorwagen had never gone farther than the end of their block.

The trip would not be easy. The roads were rutted, bumpy, rocky, and dusty. They were meant for horses, sheep, cows, and goats.

"Good," Bertha said to herself. "Hard roads will prove the Motorwagen isn't a toy."

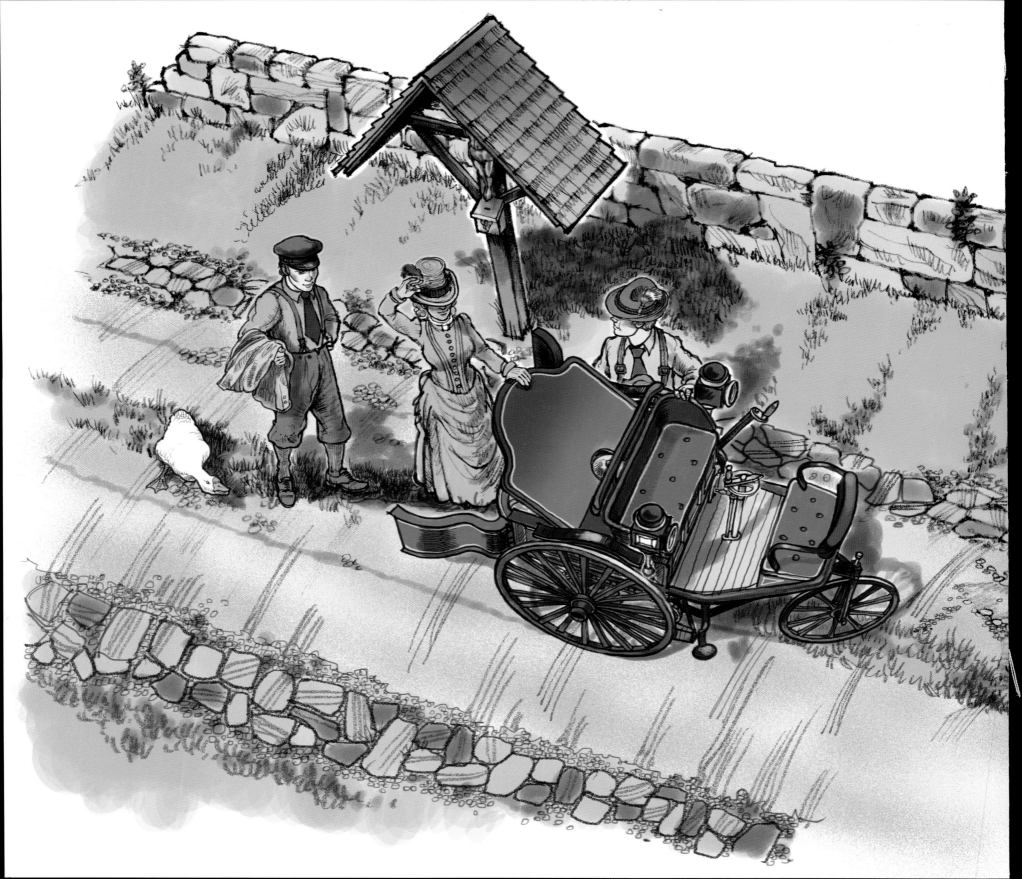

Outside their neighborhood the Motorwagen began to kick up the country dust. Bertha heard the engine wheeze before the Motorwagen shook to a stop.

Behind Bertha's seat sat the new engine built by her husband, Karl. It was tiny compared to the giant steam engines on ships and locomotives. Karl called it an "internal combustion engine."

Anyone else might be worried. But Bertha wasn't. From working in the shop with Karl, she knew that engine inside and out.

"Dust," she said to the boys. "Dust has clogged the fuel line."

Eugen and Richard watched their mother pull out the long hat pin that held her bonnet in place. She poked the pin into the fuel line to remove the dust. The fuel could flow from its tank and into the engine once again.

With each rut and rock in the road, the boys bounced in their seats. Soon they were starting up a steep hill. The Motorwagen's little engine began to shake and cough. It almost stopped.

"Out!" Bertha yelled. First the boys jumped out to lighten the load. They ran beside Bertha as she steered, but as the hill grew steeper, the engine came closer and closer to stopping.

That's when Bertha jumped out.

"Come on, boys!" she shouted. The three of them pushed with all their might.

The Motorwagen gasped to the top of the hill, at last!

Bertha and the boys leaped into their seats and rushed downhill, rattling over the bumps.

"This is fun!" squealed Richard.

As trees and bushes sped past them, Bertha added to her mental list of improvements for the next Motorwagen: "More power, better springs!"

Miles later the engine stopped without a wheeze. Cleaning the fuel line with the hat pin didn't work this time.

"Your father says a good engine *wants* to run," Bertha told the boys. "If it won't run, you just have to find the reason why it can't."

She stalked around the Motorwagen.

"*Aha!*" she said. "These rocky roads! All the shaking and bouncing has caused the wire to rub against the frame. The rubber coating around the wire has worn off."

With a grin she reached under her big skirt and took off one of the rubber garters that held up her stockings. She wrapped the rubber around the bare wire. When Bertha spun the flywheel, electricity went to the right place. The wrapping didn't let electricity escape before it traveled through the wire to the engine. They were off once again!

By now the coolness of the morning had worn off. The sunlight was warm and sweet. Richard was delighted to be carried over the landscape and past the fields and forests at a thrilling speed of nearly seven miles an hour.

"Everyone should have a Motorwagen!" Eugen called to his mother.

Bertha smiled wide and agreed.

Behind them the yellow dust raised by the whirring wheels billowed brightly. They waved to folks beside the road as dogs barked and cows mooed.

Farmers watched as the strange machine passed their beet and bean fields.

Just before they reached the next town, Wiesloch, the Motorwagen sputtered and died again. Bertha led the way to Ockler's Apothecary Shop. She asked Mr. Ockler for five liters of naphtha.

Mr. Ockler stared at her. Bertha stared back. He couldn't believe she needed that much gasoline-like fluid. He was used to selling small amounts as spot remover for clothes. "Most customers buy a bottle like this," he said.

"If you'll bring five liters of naphtha outside, Mr. Ockler, I'll show you what it's for," Bertha said.

Outside, Bertha pointed to the brass fuel tank. "Right here, Mr. Ockler."

"You're headed all the way to Pforzheim in *this*?" he asked, almost spilling the fuel.

"Yes, Mr. Ockler, and someday farther," said Bertha.

By now a small crowd had gathered. They were fascinated.

"There's no boiler? Just this tiny engine?" asked one man.

"It doesn't run on tracks, like a train?" inquired another.

"How fast will it go? Can you breathe at that speed?" asked one woman.

Bertha answered all their questions. Richard pointed out the steering handle. Eugen showed off the elm-block brakes.

With fuel in the tank, the Benzes were soon bouncing down another steep hill.

"Mama!" Eugen yelled. "We're going too fast!"

Bertha pulled back on the brake lever with all her strength. It wouldn't slow them down! She steered this way and that, barely keeping the Motorwagen on the road. The vehicle let off bitter-smelling smoke as it rocked from side to side.

"What's that smell?" Richard asked.

"The brakes," Bertha said. "So much friction builds up heat. The wooden blocks that press against the wheel have been worn smooth, so they slip and smoke instead of stopping the axle from spinning."

When the steep hill turned to flat ground, they finally slowed to a halt. The boys watched their mother take the wooden brake blocks off the Motorwagen. She got a local shoemaker to nail thick, rough leather to them. Leather prevented the brake blocks from slipping against the wheel rims. Bertha had invented brake linings! They were off again.

The sun was close to setting when they drove into the village of
Pforzheim and right up to the door of Bertha's mother's house.

"Bertha, my dear! And my boys!" her mother cried. "What a surprise!"

"We've driven Karl's marvelous Motorwagen from Mannheim to see you,
Mama. We've had a lovely drive," Bertha explained.

"In that thing?" her mother asked in horror.

"Oh yes," Bertha said easily. "It wasn't difficult."

Richard and Eugen looked at each other and grinned. Was their mother kidding?

"You'll see," Bertha added. "Other people will be driving up to your door in Benz Motorwagens quite soon."

"I hope not this evening," her mother said firmly.

While the boys were eating up Grandma's soup, Bertha walked to the village telegraph office and sent a sweet note to Karl. She knew he had to be worried.

Bertha also sent telegrams to newspapers. Those newspapers told other newspapers. The story of her journey made its way to Berlin, Paris, and Rome. Excited headlines about Bertha's drive were traveling faster than the Motorwagen—all over the world!

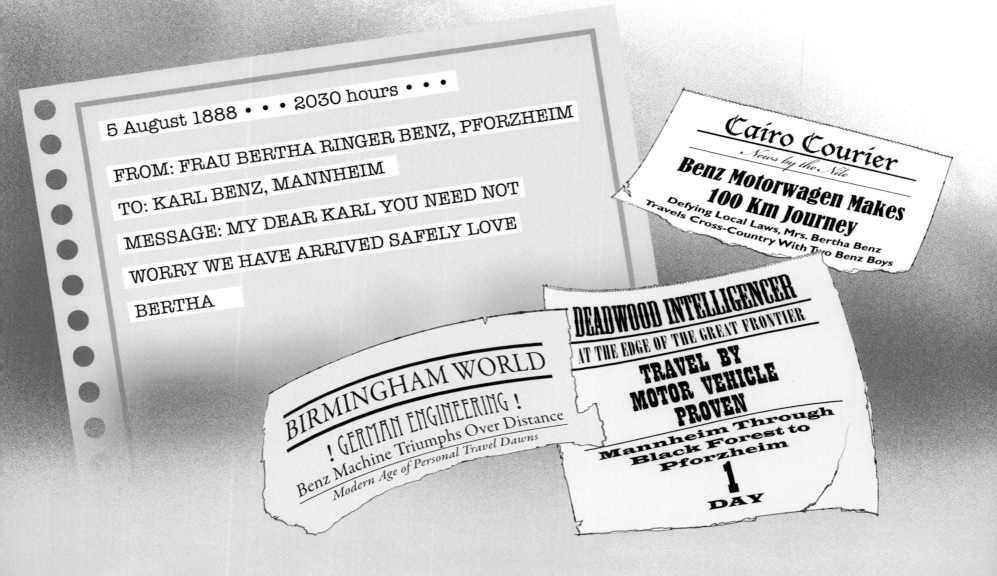

5 August 1888 • • • 2030 hours • • •

FROM: FRAU BERTHA RINGER BENZ, PFORZHEIM

TO: KARL BENZ, MANNHEIM

MESSAGE: MY DEAR KARL YOU NEED NOT WORRY WE HAVE ARRIVED SAFELY LOVE

BERTHA

Cairo Courier
News by the Nile

Benz Motorwagen Makes 100 Km Journey
Defying Local Laws, Mrs. Bertha Benz
Travels Cross-Country With Two Benz Boys

BIRMINGHAM WORLD
! GERMAN ENGINEERING !
Benz Machine Triumphs Over Distance
Modern Age of Personal Travel Dawns

DEADWOOD INTELLIGENCER
AT THE EDGE OF THE GREAT FRONTIER

TRAVEL BY MOTOR VEHICLE PROVEN

Mannheim Through Black Forest to Pforzheim

1 DAY

Emperor Wilhelm II liked reading stories about brilliant German engineering. He told the policemen outside the Benzes' shop to go home. Church officials decided that if a woman and her boys could use the Teufelwagen to visit Grandma, perhaps it wasn't so evil after all.

Karl was proud of his wife and grateful that she was brave enough to show their family—and the world—what his Motorwagen could do.

Bertha didn't think she had done anything especially extraordinary. She had taken her boys for a ride in the marvelous Motorwagen.

"Karl," Bertha explained, "it was simply time to take a drive."

AUTOMOBILE EVOLUTION

1898: French industrialist Louis Renault's Voiturette, or "Little Car," appears and is made in several models through 1903.

1914: During World War I, the British firm Rolls-Royce, originally known for its luxury cars, supplies armored cars to British troops. T. E. Lawrence, "Lawrence of Arabia," uses several against the Turks in the Arabian Desert.

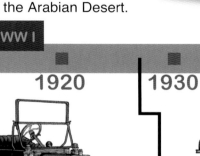

1939: Adolf Hitler tasks racing-car designer Ferdinand Porsche to design the Volkswagen, the "People's Car," as affordable transportation for everyone. But the simple, beautiful VW Beetle isn't mass-produced until after 1945, at the end of WWII.

1888: Bertha takes a drive!

1880	1890	1900	1910	1920	1930	1940	1950

WW I   WW II

1902: Former American carriage-maker Clement Studebaker produces elegant electric runabouts in several models through 1912 before reluctantly shifting to more practical gasoline engines.

1908: Henry Ford's Model T is the first widely affordable automobile in the US, sturdy and available in "any color as long as it's black." 14.6 million are made between 1908 and 1927.

1941: The American Bantam Car Company pioneers the first Jeep, a four-wheel-drive, all-purpose vehicle for the US Army. Thousands are produced during World War II. After the war, they create a market for off-road vehicles.

1769: French inventor Nicolas-Joseph Cugnot builds the Cugnot-Brezin "steam dray" wagon, which weighs 2.5 tons and achieves 2.5 mph (3.6 kph). When it runs out of control and knocks down a wall, the first car accident is recorded.

1928: In Indianapolis, IN, the Duesenberg Model J is built to compete with European luxury cars. It reaches 119 mph (191.5 kph) but is so expensive only movie stars and tycoons can afford it.

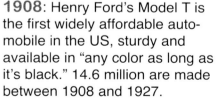

1948: Paris Mondial de l'Automobile engineers the Citroën 2CV (Deux Chevaux, or "Two Horses") to mobilize rural French citizens. Seven million are made between 1948 and 1989.

1987: Sunraycer, a solar-powered race car, is designed by the brilliant Paul MacCready to compete in the world's first race for solar-powered cars (now called the World Solar Challenge). The race runs between Darwin and Adelaide, Australia—1,867 miles (3,005 km). With an average speed of 41.6 mph (66.9 kph), the Sunraycer wins by an enormous margin.

2008: The Tesla Roadster is the first highway-legal electric car to use lithium-ion battery cells, offer sports-car performance, and include a battery range of more than 200 miles (320 km) per charge. Like the Duesenberg Model J, the price of the Tesla Roadster is out of reach for all but the wealthy.

1960   1970   1980   1990   **2000**   2010   2020   2030

1951: Nash Motors of Kenosha, WI, produces the Nash Rambler convertible during a time when dozens of US car manufacturers are active post-war. Eventually, huge corporations buy out most manufacturers, and the number of American automakers diminishes.

1990: Paul MacCready designs General Motors' battery electric EV1 in response to California's Low Emissions Vehicle (LEV) rule, meant to phase out "dirty" engines and encourage new designs for cleaner-running cars. But in 2003, the LEV rule falls victim to lobbying by automotive and oil corporations. GM recalls and destroys all EV1s.

AFTER 2000: The automobile continues to change our society. Cars and highways determine where we live, how we work, and how our cities grow or fail. Long commutes, enormous traffic jams, parking difficulty, and air pollution frustrate many of us. Some suggest that computer-driven cars will be the future. Perhaps we won't "own" cars but "call" them for a ride? A few driverless cars are already on the road today as proof-of-concept tests, including Google's self-driving car project.

AND INTO TOMORROW: What would Bertha and Karl Benz invent today? What innovative transportation for tomorrow might they envision? What challenges might stir Bertha's imagination, courage, and curiosity? What does your imagination see?

THE BENZ MOTORWAGEN III

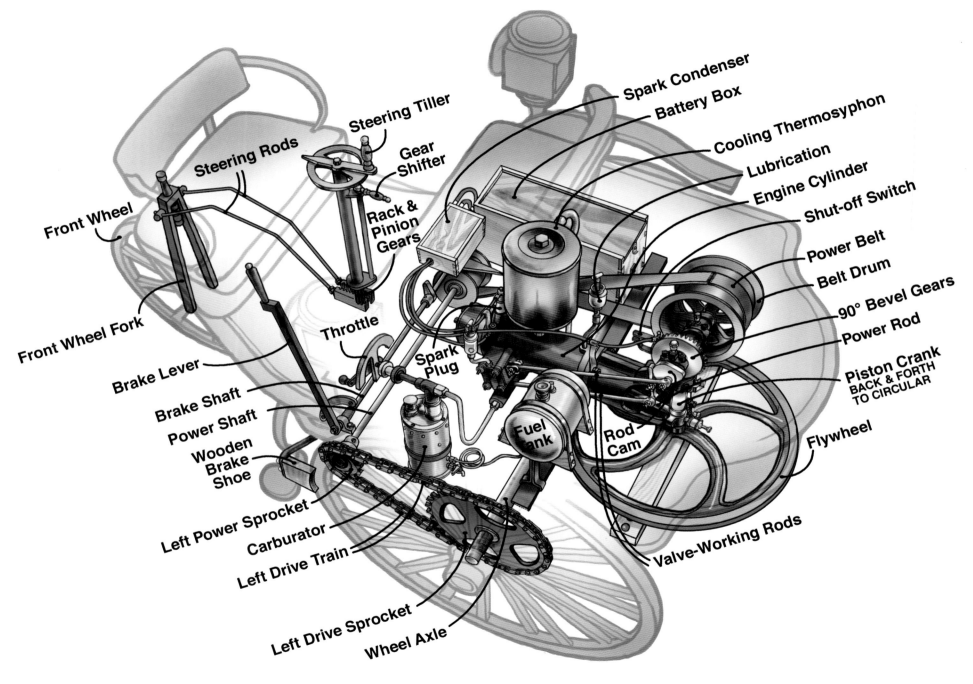

Steering Tiller

Steering Rods

Gear Shifter

Front Wheel

Rack & Pinion Gears

Front Wheel Fork

Throttle

Brake Lever

Spark Plug

Brake Shaft

Power Shaft

Wooden Brake Shoe

Left Power Sprocket

Carburator

Left Drive Train

Left Drive Sprocket

Wheel Axle

Spark Condenser

Battery Box

Cooling Thermosyphon

Lubrication

Engine Cylinder

Shut-off Switch

Power Belt

Belt Drum

90° Bevel Gears

Power Rod

Piston Crank
BACK & FORTH
TO CIRCULAR

Flywheel

Valve-Working Rods

Fuel Tank

Rod Cam

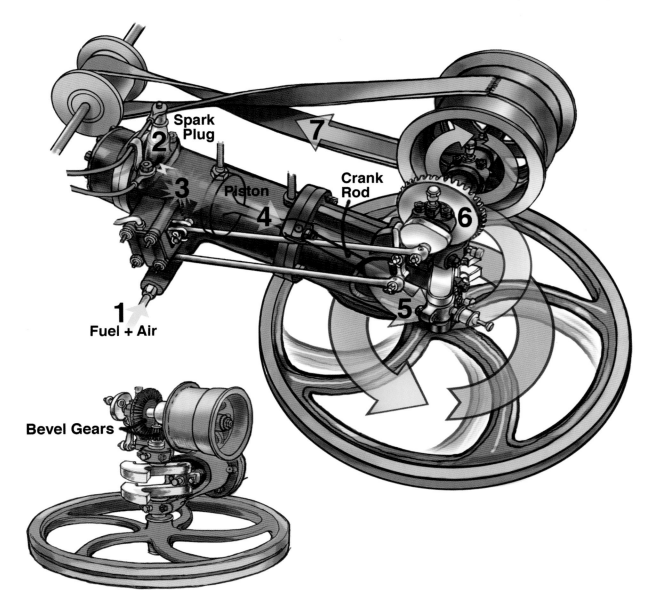

Spark Plug

Crank Rod

Piston

Fuel + Air

Bevel Gears

1 Mixture of fuel and air is drawn into the piston chamber.
2 Spark plug ignites fuel-air mixture.
3 Burning mixture expands, pushing piston head.
4 Crank rod linked to piston converts back-and-forth motion to spin.
5 Flywheel and gears spin vertical drive shaft.
6 Bevel gears convert vertical spin into belt drum's horizontal spin.
7 Leather belt turns second drum connected to driving wheels.

LOOKING BACK, WRITING FORWARD

How difficult it is to write—and illustrate—the flavor and reality of lives from more than a century ago!

Is it possible to re-create Bertha Benz's view of the world? She lived in a world we can never walk through. Most of it was rural land full of farmers and herdsmen, with only a few cities that were like industrial islands. Electric lights were rare. Women's lives were restricted, dependent on family or husbands. Children's lives were not carefree, and often, because of childhood diseases, tragically short.

And yet society was changing during Bertha's life (1849–1944) because of new, powerful technology: the telegraph, railroads, and steamships. Common people were just beginning to move around. A middle-class family might take the train to the seashore or the mountains. Emigrants from war-torn countries could book cheap steerage passage across the Atlantic to North or South America. News from impossibly distant countries arrived by telegraph. A sense of the world's real size and diversity was part of a new consciousness.

That big world was frightening to many, even Kaiser Wilhelm. From our perch in today's world, it sounds silly that he and the church banned the Benz Motorwagen. But churchmen and emperors feared independent people who wanted to change old comfortable rules. They feared that independent people would want to govern themselves and choose their own leaders, and might even refuse to fight for squabbling kings. Change is seldom comfy.

Change, however, excited Bertha Benz. She was brave, sensible, and strong. She was a businesswoman, mechanic, inventor, and revolutionary. She astonished the world on her monumental trip across difficult country in an unproven invention—her Motorwagen. On this journey with her boys (Eugen was age fifteen, and Richard was fourteen), she met every problem with a calm sensibility. And when she drove into her mother's yard in Pforzheim, she had accomplished a true adventure. She was a hero. The only reason we haven't heard more about her is that heroic women often go unnoticed.

Describing her journey for you has made me very happy, even though it has been exceptionally difficult to get Bertha's adventure as close to the real story as I can. No one wrote down Bertha's words, so I've imagined what the mother and explorer I've come to know might have said.

At times, researching this book was confusing. Most accounts of Bertha's journey (you can see a few on YouTube) show her traveling in the first model of the Benz Motorwagen, the BMW I. That was the very first car. But Bertha made her famous trip in the Benz Motorwagen III, a more refined machine. Discovering how it worked and how it was put together has been tricky. There are no measured drawings or widely shared reproductions of the BMW III. I've done my best to interpret the BMW III from a few dozen good photos of the original.

It was difficult, but you're worth it. Young readers deserve the truth. Details count. And while I'm not at all certain that my illustrations accurately show every precise detail of Bertha's world, including her beloved engines, gears, belts, and levers, everything has been drawn with diligent research and great respect. What I hope Bertha would appreciate most is the book's admiration for her toughness, intelligence, and vision. I wish I'd known her. Don't you?